Ida Bohatta

A Day with Heinzel

English Version by John Theobald

ars edition

Six O'Clock

"Six o'clock and time to rise!
How beautiful to wake
For breakfast, brush the hair from your eyes,
And leap into the lake!"
But Hummel turned over half asleep
And mumbled it would be
Twice as beautiful to let it keep
And wake in time for tea.

Seven O'Clock

Why are things so upside down?
It really makes you stop
That every time we get hot sun,
The shower hardly gives a drop;
And when we all are frozen stiff
By wintry days, behold!
Down comes the rain from a laden leaf
In icicles shivery cold.

Eight O'Clock

In a grove in the land of the fairies' home
The bumble bee gets along fine.
There's plenty to eat for herself and the gnome
Both at breakfast and when they dine.
The news of Heinzel's grove spreads wide,
And now all day without rest,
The busy bees fly in from outside
And settle down for a feast.

Nine O'Clock

It's a bore to be brave when you're small;
It only spoils the fun:
I shouldn't be going to the dentist at all,
For the pain in my tooth is gone.
But I had an appointment at nine,
And here's a little riddle:
I showed up right on the dot just fine –
With a pain instead in my middle.

Ten O'Clock

At every good turn you do for free,
If even only when
You save the life of a drowning bee,
A secret clock strikes ten.
Then think whether even once, as you bore
In your heart that secret clock,
Through all the last seven days or more,
You acted so it struck.

Eleven O'Clock

Now I understand why bees
Pay their visits in such haste,
Stopping off just as they please,
Only pausing for a taste.
Every time they break their journey,
That's to see if Heinzel's there,
Who, when he prepares the honey,
Flavors it with fairy fare.

Twelve O'Clock

If I could change the way of the world,
I'd fasten time with a patent lock,
So all the hours were bunched and furled
Upright to make it twelve o'clock.
This would be fine, because at noon,
When bees and gnomes all pause for soup,
The day would stop, we'd eat, and soon
The same sweet lunch hour would come up.

One O'Clock

The day's still here and I am weary;
Beside me even sleeps a bee.
Let me just pretend the dreary
Work's all done and I am free:
Free to sleep, and this pretending
Makes the labor only seem
Busy till the long day's ending,
Happy – since it's all a dream.

Two to Two-Fifteen

"Give us only these short minutes,
Shut inside our fragrant prison,
Longing to be like the linnets,
Flying to the far horizon."

"Fair flower, we can only tell you
That your sweet bouquets are given
With a longing to be like you,
Shut inside a flower's heaven."

Five to Five-Thirty

"What a lovely tune that is!
Can't you play another one?
Just for half-an-hour, please,
While we cool off in the sun?"

"Oh, I'll play it more than once,"
Heinzel said to those small pests,
"Just to make mosquitoes dance
Longer, and thus bite me less."

Six-Forty-Five

"You come home every evening later.
How can you stand to work so hard?
Take off your shoes, sit back – that's better!
Now soak your feet. You must be tired!"

My bee just smiles and murmurs low,
"We have a secret about this:
Except for stinging, all we do
Is done for other people's bliss."

Ten O'Clock

Once again the day is done:
The blessed shining of the sun,
Fragrance of flowers – all joy – is flown.
I want to cry because it's gone.
Yet I am happy, I must own.
I think of it and feel no sorrow,
Because, when morning has begun,
There'll be a beautiful tomorrow.

Books by Ida Bohatta

Bow Wow
Doctor Allsgood
Heinzel the Innkeeper
The Merry Hoppers
Shooting Stars
The Misjudged Mushroom
Barli the Ice Bear
A Day with Heinzel
The Cloud Kitchen
Velvet Paws
The Brown Family
All of the Birds

Wulli and Susi
Wixi the Easter Rabbit
The Helpful Dwarfs
Raindrops
Flipp and Flirr
The Hardworking Bee
Little Men Underground
The Busy Savers
Ice Men
The Little Advent Book
Winter House
Saint Nicholas